Roundy & Friends
Book Seven

Andres Varela

Illustrations and Graphic Design by Carlos F. González
Co-Producer Germán Hernández
Third Edition
© 2019 Soccertowns® LLC

After a long journey from Galveston, Texas, through Kansas City, Chicago, Columbus, Washington D.C. and Philadelphia the group is on their way to New York City.

They cross from Pennsylvania to New Jersey and see the sign "Welcome to New Jersey the Garden State", then crossed the state line into New York and see the sign "Welcome to New York the Empire State".

The City of New York is the most populous city in the United States. The city consists of five boroughs, which make up the five different areas of New York City.

The boroughs are Manhattan, Bronx, Queens, Brooklyn and Staten Island. The population in the five boroughs is approximately 8.1 Million people, but in the whole New York City Metropolitan area the population is over 20 Million.

Teo explains: "Manhattan is the one of the most famous places in the World, and what you may not know is that Manhattan is an island."

Roundy replies, "How is it an island? It's not in the middle of the ocean".

Teo responds, "It is an island because it is surrounded by water on all of its sides. The rivers East, Hudson and Harlem surround the island."

Because Manhattan is surrounded by rivers, there are many bridges and tunnels connecting the island to the main land.

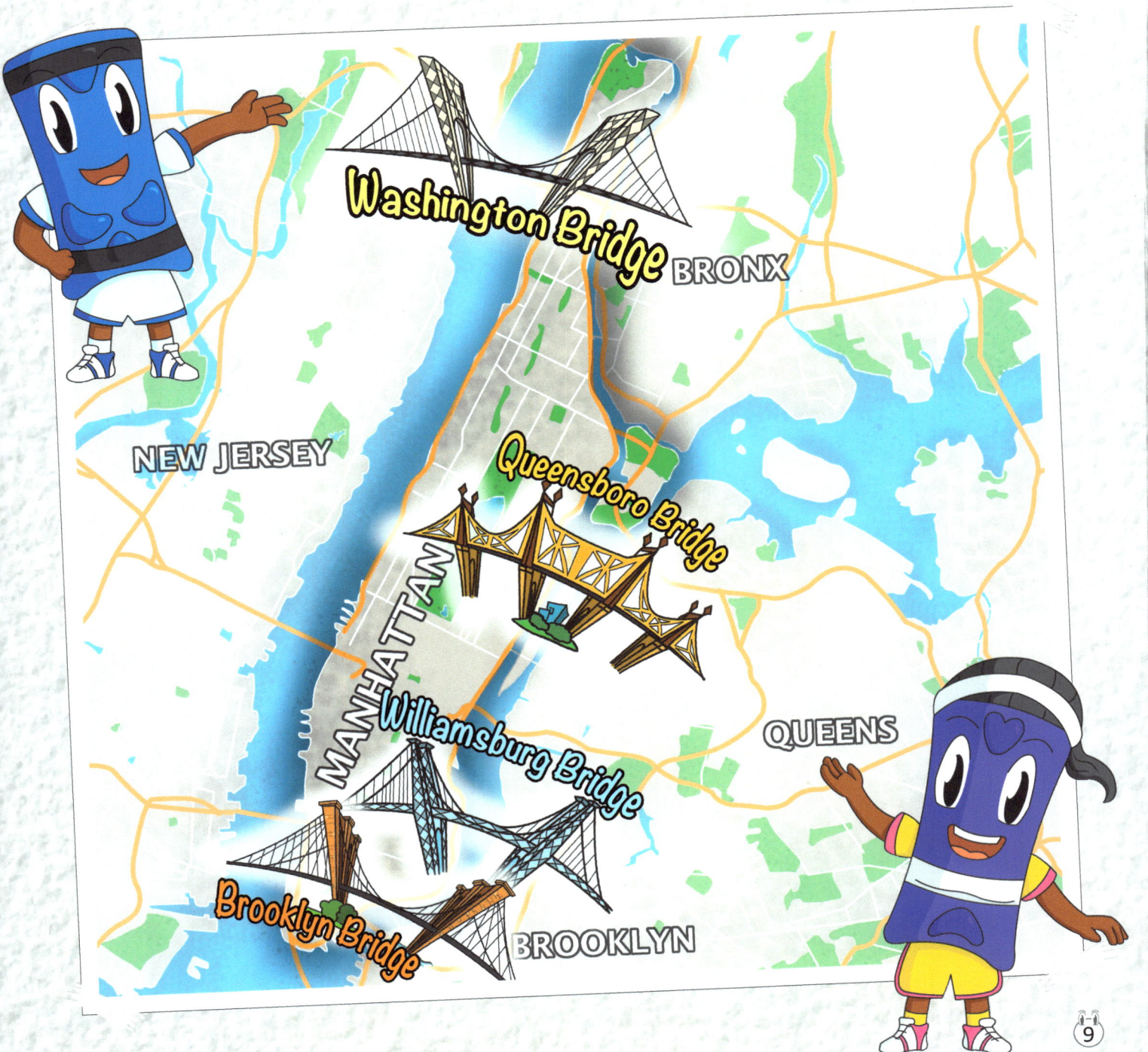

Teo tells the team: "There are many places to visit in New York City, but we won't have time to go to all of them during this trip, so I'm sure we will come back in the future."

Teo opens up a map and shows the team the route they will take to visit the many exciting places in New York City. The tour starts at the Empire State Building, then continues on to the Chrysler building, Times Square, Central Park, the Intrepid Sea, Air & Space Museum, and finally the Statue of Liberty.

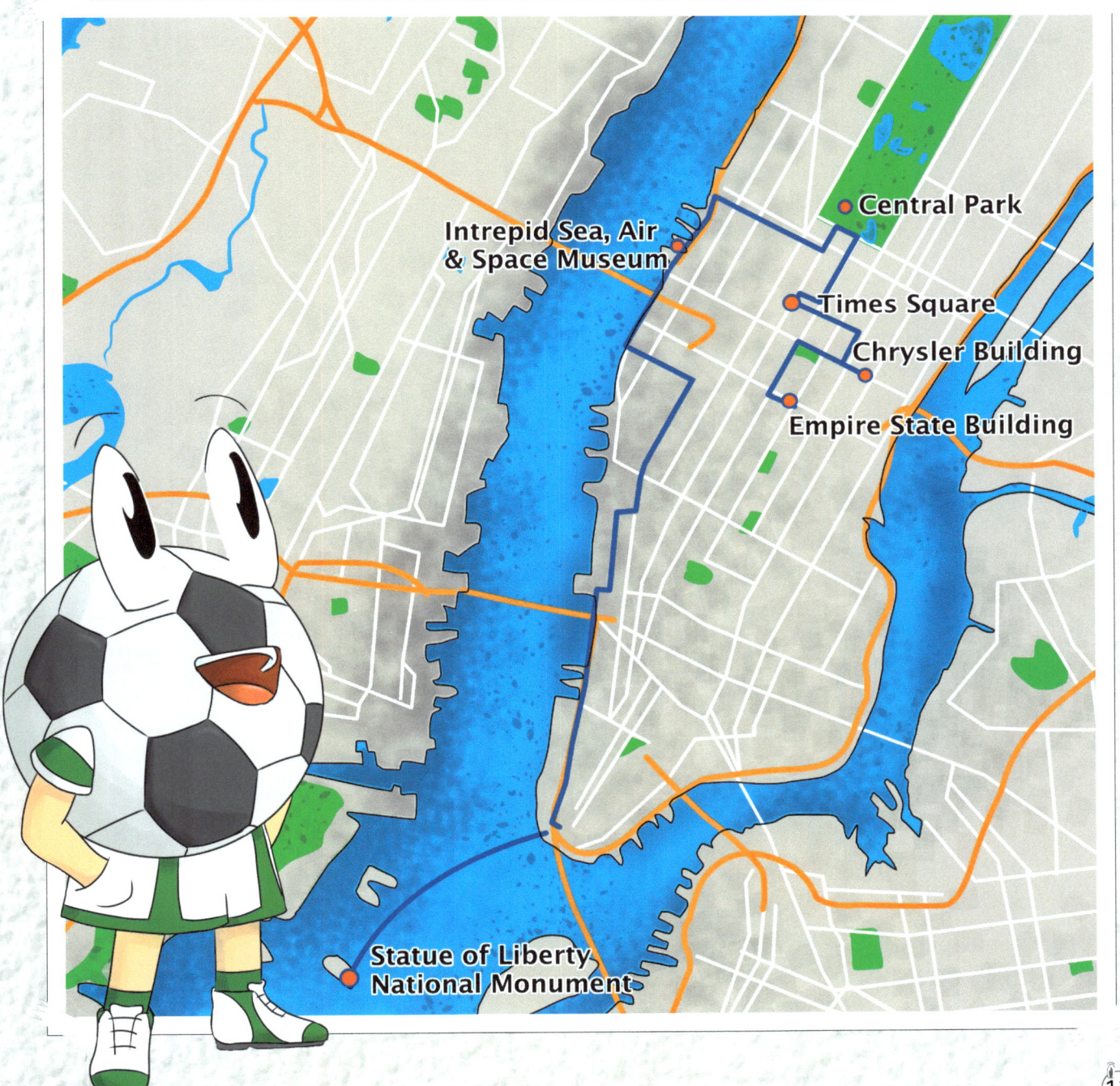

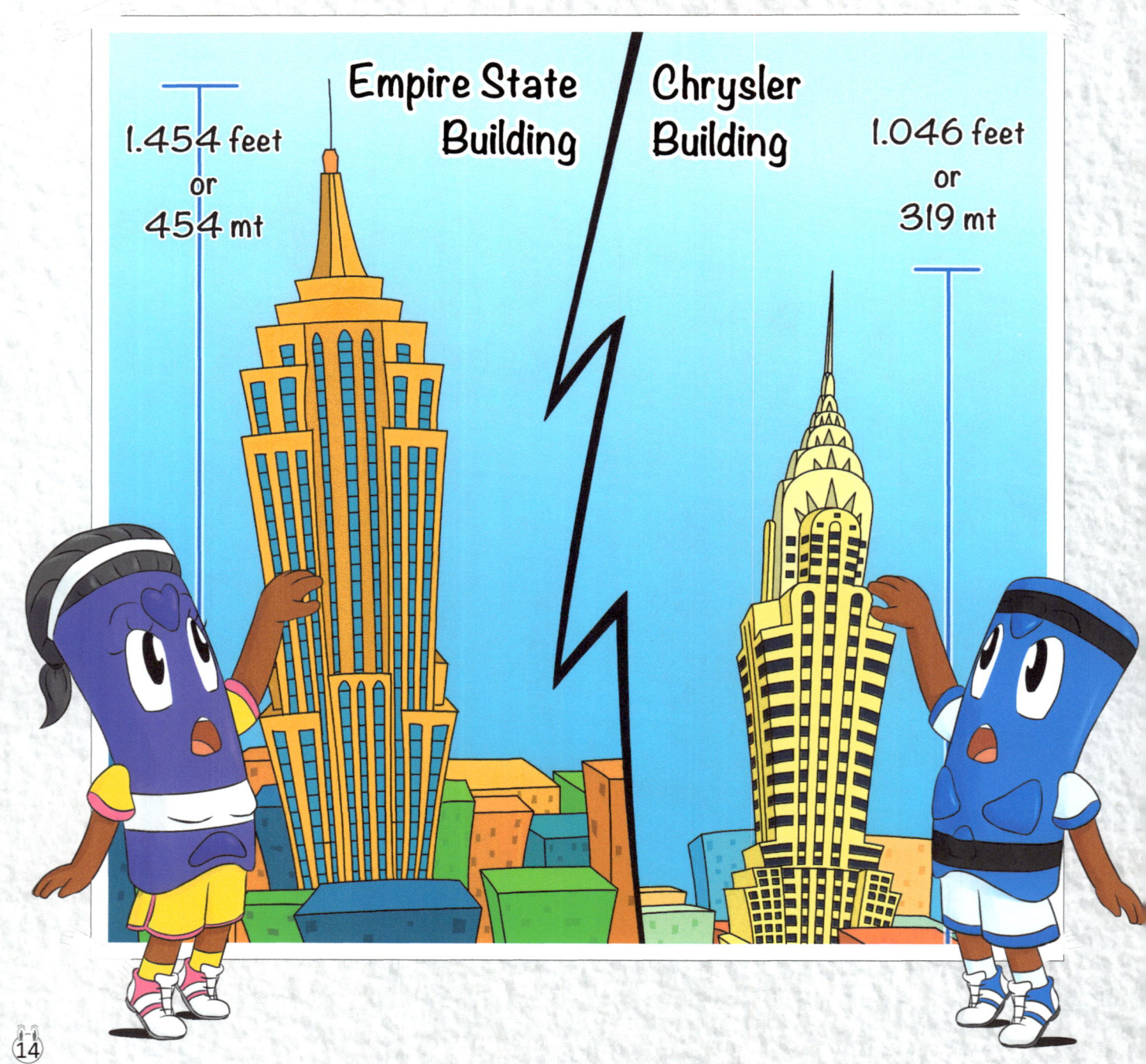

The construction of the Empire State building was completed in 1931 and it took only 410 days from start to finish, that is just over 13 months. The building is 1,454 feet or 454 meters tall. It was the tallest building in the world from 1931 to 1970 until the World Trade Center Towers were built. Construction on the Chrysler building started in 1928 and it was completed in May 1930. The Chrysler building is 1,046 feet or 319 meters tall. Once completed the building was the tallest in the world until the Empire State building was inaugurated.

Times Square is a name that refers to an area in Manhattan that is one of the busiest intersections in the world. Over 50 Million people walk this intersection on a yearly basis, which is over 325,000 pedestrians every day.

The team is amazed at the amount of bright signs in Time Square and the amount of people and cars. It is a beautiful place to see people from all walks of life, do some shopping and have a nice meal.

The next morning they wake up bright and early and head to Central Park, the biggest urban park in the United States, which means the biggest park within a city in the US.
The park is 843 acres or 8.41 km2, this means it is a very large park where people can enjoy time away from the busy streets and buildings of Manhattan.

Inside of Central Park there is a zoo. A volunteer at the zoo gives tours. The zoo is home to lots of animals, including bears, penguins, polar bears and many others. Zoos are a lot of fun!

After the Central Park Zoo the team heads out to the Intrepid Sea, Air and Space Museum.

Teo tells them: "The USS Intrepid is an aircraft carrier, built during World War II. What really amazed me when I came to see it the first time, was how much history the ship has from participating in several war battles and rescuing space ships such as Mercury or Gemini."

There are many other things to see in the museum, including a submarine, a space shuttle and one of the Concorde planes, which holds the fastest record for crossing the Atlantic ocean in under 3 hours, when a normal airplane takes over 6 hours.

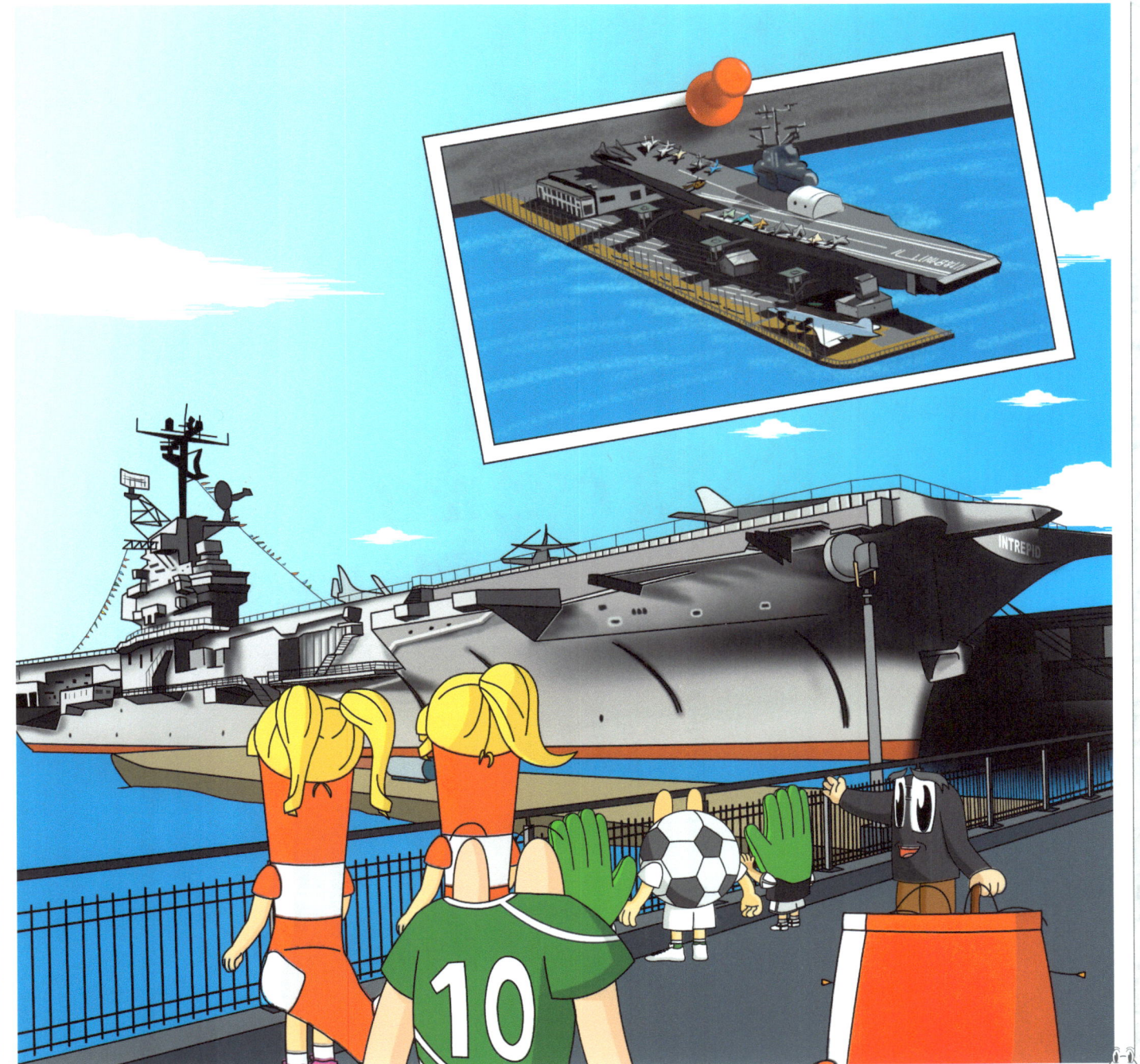

After learning so much history at the Intrepid Museum they head south to the Ferry that takes them to the Statue of Liberty.

The Statue of Liberty was a gift given to the people of the United States from France. It was dedicated on October 28th, 1886. The Statue represents the Roman Goddess Libertas who wears a robe, while holding a torch and a tablet, evoking the ideals of freedom and welcoming people arriving from other countries. The tablet is etched with the date of the United States Independence, July 4th, 1776.

After visiting the impressive Statue of Liberty the group heads north then west to New Jersey, crossing under the Hudson river through the Holland Tunnel.

Once in New Jersey, they continue heading North towards Bear Mountain State Park.

Bear Mountain is a beautiful park close to New York City. It is about one hour and twenty minutes North of Manhattan. The park has amazing views of the Hudson River and its surroundings. During the fall the leaves on the trees change colors making it a great attraction for pictures and artists.

After Bear mountain the team heads South West towards the Tappan Zee Bridge.

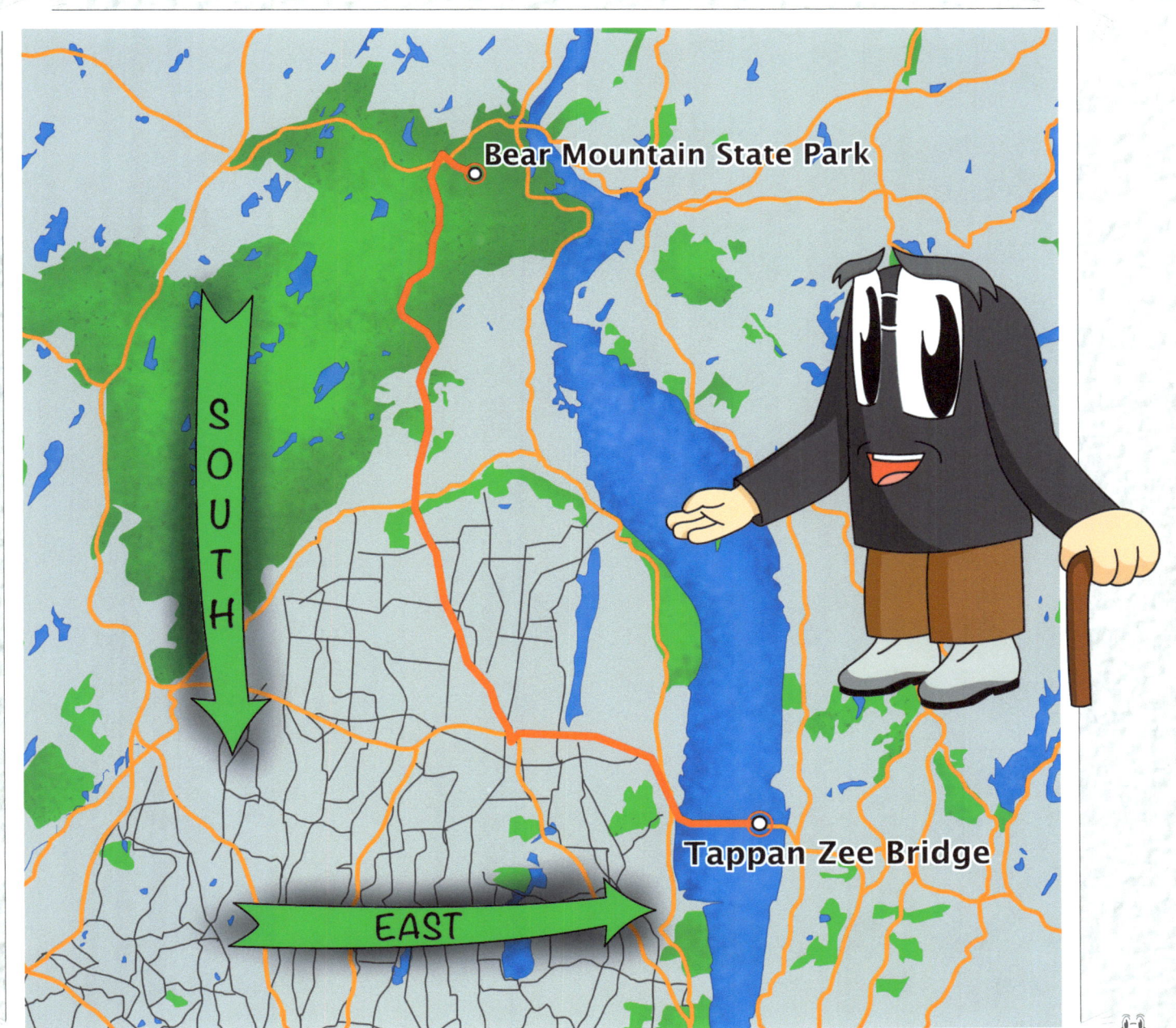

This bridge was opened on December 15th, 1955. It crosses over the Hudson River. The length of the bridge is 16,013 feet or 4,881 meters. On average, over 134,000 vehicles cross the bridge every day.

Come back and read the next story, we're heading to Boston.....

www.ingramcontent.com/pod-product-compliance
Lightning Source LLC
Chambersburg PA
CBHW041500220426
43661CB00016B/1205